CHICAGO
BULLS

CHICAGO
BULLS

TOM PETERSON

CREATIVE EDUCATION

Photo Credit: Creative Education would like to thank NBA photographer Ron Koch (New York City) for the color photography in this series.

Published by Creative Education Inc., 123 South Broad Street, Mankato, Minnesota 56001.

ISBN: 0-88682-199-1

Michael "Air" Jordan was elated when he learned that he had been drafted by the Chicago Bulls, in spite of the fact that the Bulls were floundering at the time.

"Ever since my first visit to Chicago," Jordan said, "I've felt that the place has this incredible energy. It's big, but the people aren't phony or stuck-up, they're for real. I feel very much at home in Chicago, like I'm finally plugged into the right current."

When a live wire like Jordan gets plugged in, watch out. During his first four years in the league, the high-flying No. 23 shattered virtually every Chicago offensive record. Jordan and Wilt Chamberlain are the only players ever to score more than 3,000 points in a single season. But no one, not even Chamberlain, could excite a basketball crowd in quite the same way as Jordan does today.

To truly appreciate the good times that Chicago basketball fans are enjoying today, we must first relive some tough times they endured in years gone by.

Our story begins in 1925, the year pro basketball took its first step toward big league stature with the formation of the old American Basketball League. Chicago's entry, the Bruins, drew small crowds over the next five years. To be quite honest, pro basketball was pretty sleepy stuff during the 1920s. Games of this era ended in such typical scores as 29-23, 26-25 and 31-27. When the Chicago Bruins folded with the rest of the ABL in 1931, league officials blamed the downfall on the Great Depression, but the true cause was its lack of fans.

Pro basketball staged a brief, but flashy, comeback in Chicago at the end of World War II. Two rival pro circuits, the National Basketball League and the Basketball Association of America, were battling each other for supremacy.

In 1946, the Chicago Gears of the NBL signed the most popular college player of the day, George Mikan. The 6-foot-10 Mikan stimulated interest in the pro game. Famous for his hook shots, his thick glasses and his No. 99, Mikan was the greatest player of his time.

Unfortunately for Chicago, the Gears folded immediately after Mikan led the team to the 1946-47 NBL championship.

A ferocious competitor, Jerry Sloan gave the Bulls all-out intensity, and he expected the same from his teammates.

Meanwhile, the Basketball Association of America had been trying its own luck by launching a franchise in the Windy City. The team was called the Chicago Stags and it played well enough during its first season, 1946-47, to win the Western Division and finish second to Philadelphia for the BAA title.

At the season opener in New York's Madison Square Garden, the Stags played to a crowd of more than 17,000 fans. Despite the team's success, the Stags had a difficult time drawing respectable crowds at home. At the time, Chicago's sports fans seemed to be preoccupied with the White Sox and Bears.

In 1949-50, the NBL and BAA merged to become the modern day National Basketball Association. The Chicago Stags played just one year in the NBA before the team folded.

Eleven years later, in 1961, Chicago was awarded a second NBA team. This new club was called the Packers because its homecourt, the Amphitheater, was located near the world famous Chicago stockyards. As the new team in the league, the Packers had the first pick in the college draft and immediately chose Walt Bellamy, a 6-foot-11 center from Indiana. Bellamy averaged an astonishing 30.6 points per game that year, second only to Wilt Chamberlain in the entire NBA.

Airborne Walt Bellamy (8) of the Chicago Packers displays the all-out determination that characterized his NBA career. (1961)

But even with an exciting player like Bellamy, the Packers were unable to draw many fans. In 1962-63, they changed their name to the Chicago Zephyrs and moved to a smaller arena. There they desperately tried to lure more fans, but a losing record spoiled the effort. At season's end, the owners called it quits. The Zephyrs moved to Baltimore where the team was renamed the Bullets. Once again, Chicago found itself without a pro basketball club.

The NBA had already watched two of its teams go down to failure in Chicago, but no one in the league was ready to accept the idea that one of America's biggest cities might be unable to support major league basketball. So in 1966 the NBA tried again, and the third time was the charm.

Once again, the decision was made to identify the club with Chicago's famous livestock market. Thus, the team was named the Bulls. John Kerr was installed as head coach of the new club.

By choosing Jerry Sloan of Baltimore as their No. 1 pick in the NBA expansion draft, the Bulls picked up an inspirational leader who would spark the team and define its playing style through the next ten seasons.

Jerry Sloan

Some said Sloan couldn't cut it in the pro ranks. But Jerry Sloan was not a quitter.

Sloan was a local talent, raised in Southern Illinois. As a swingman at Evansville University, he had led the Purple Aces to two national championships. Still, nothing came easy for him. Too small for forward and too slow for guard, he knew he would have to work very hard to come out a winner in the NBA.

The Baltimore Bullets had originally drafted him in the first round of the 1965 collegiate draft, but they kept him on the bench. Some said Sloan couldn't cut it in the pro ranks. But Jerry Sloan was not a quitter. When the Bulls made him their first choice, he vowed to repay them with all-out hustle.

Bob Boozer

Dick Motta, who would become the Bulls head coach after Kerr, marvelled at the way Sloan hustled. "Jerry was not physically gifted," said Motta, "but he used to set goals for every game that would help his team win. For instance, he would get eight rebounds, even playing in the backcourt. He would take three charges, come up with three loose balls and hold his man ten points under his average. By doing those things he had contributed to his team in many ways."

Everyone in Chicago expected the Bulls to lose big in their first season. Only 4,200 fans showed up for Chicago's 1966-67 home opener against the powerful San Francisco Warriors, but the small crowd was treated to a delightful surprise. Sloan sizzled for a game high 26 points and the Bulls defeated the Warriors, 119-116.

As the Bulls' charter season wore on, more and more fans discovered the team. Sloan and his backcourt partner Guy Rodgers were the backbone of the team.

In his first year . . . Rodgers would lead the team in scoring and the entire NBA in assists.

Rodgers was a nine-year veteran who had previously been Wilt Chamberlain's set-up man with the San Francisco Warriors. When Wilt had established the all-time NBA single game scoring record of 100 points, Rodgers had contributed 20 assists. In his first year with the Bulls, Rodgers would lead the team in scoring and the entire NBA in assists.

Jerry Sloan drives the baseline past the Bucks' Kareem Abdul Jabbar for two of the 10,233 career points he scored for Chicago.

During the stretch drive to the playoffs, the Bulls really came into their own. They won eight of their last 12 games, including a victory over Wilt Chamberlain's 76ers that clinched a playoff berth for Chicago. Although the Sixers would eventually go on to win the NBA title that year, Chicago received nearly as much publicity. By making the playoffs in their very first season of operation, the Bulls had become the most successful expansion team ever.

But Chicago started out with a thud in 1967-68, losing 15 of its first 16 games after moving to their new home, Chicago Stadium. The team was still reeling from the loss of forward Don Kojis and back-up center George Wilson in the May 1967 expansion draft. Jimmy Washington and McCoy McLemore eventually filled their shoes, however, and the Bulls recovered in time to make the playoffs.

Convinced the team could improve their play, the owners searched for a new head coach for the next season. The hiring of Dick Motta, a virtual unknown, was a surprise to everyone throughout the league.

Motta was quite a bit different from the average NBA coach. He had never played college or pro ball, and he had actually been cut from his high school varsity team during his senior year. After high school, Motta had decided to skip college, stay home and be a farmer. When a friend finally convinced him to enroll at Utah State, Motta did try out for the basketball team, but he was cut four years in a row.

Dick Motta, was named head coach of the Bulls in 1968, and NBA Coach of the Year in 1970-71.

Things didn't get any easier after college. When Motta applied for the head coaching position at Idaho's Twin Falls High, the school turned him down. Motta finally landed a coaching position at Weber State in Utah. There he clinched three conference titles over the next six years.

Of course, college ball is one thing, and the NBA is quite another. When Motta showed up for his first day of practice with the Bulls, he knew he would have to prove himself all over again.

Motta's volatile coaching style had a way of uniting the Chicago players and fans. In time, the Bulls became a team known for its floor burns, flare-ups and hustle. With Motta riding the officials and Jerry Sloan fighting for loose balls, there was seldom a dull moment. The Bulls were fun to watch even when they weren't winning.

During Motta's first four seasons, the Bulls' record improved each year. The coach's strategy was to grind the opposition's offense to a standstill. Three times during Motta's seven-year reign Chicago proved itself the toughest defensive unit in the NBA.

Looking back over Motta's first few years with the Bulls, it's important to note that some clever trades were made. As a result, Chicago received the nucleus of what would soon become one of the most exciting teams in the NBA. From Milwaukee came a balding, misfit guard named Bobby Weiss and a skinny reserve named Bob Love. All-Star forward Chet Walker came from Philadelphia, and centers Walt Wesley and Bob Kauffman came from Cincinnati and Seattle, respectively.

Nicknamed "Chet the Jet," Walker was paired with Love upfront while Weiss backed up Sloan and Clem Haskins in the backcourt. Wesley, Kauffman and Tom Boerwinkle took turns in the pivot. The new Bulls leaped to third in the Western Division, their best record ever, and back into the playoffs.

As a result, Chicago received the nucleus of what would soon become one of the most exciting teams in the NBA.

Motta's mastery continued in 1970-71. The club didn't use any flashy plays or complicated strategy, they just played basic basketball. It allowed Chicago to run up an impressive 51-31 record, good enough for a second place finish behind Milwaukee in the Midwest Division.

Though Chicago was finally eliminated in Game 7 of the first round of the playoffs, Motta received well deserved recognition by being voted the NBA Coach of the Year.

Just before the next season began, Motta made another important trade, this time for Norm Van Lier. A shrewd playmaker and fierce competitor, Van Lier went by the nickname "Stormin' Norman."

Oddly enough, back in 1969 Chicago had traded Van Lier to Cincinnati after picking him up in the college draft. At that time Motta thought that the frail looking, 6-foot-1 guard was too small to make it in the NBA. But after witnessing Van Lier's fierce defensive play, Motta changed his mind.

What Van Lier brought to the Bulls was blazing speed, all-out defense, and the keen ability to spot the open man. He was a hardnosed player who often gave the skin off his knees and elbows for the team.

With Van Lier on board, the Bulls threatened to make it past the first round of the NBA playoffs in 1972-73. But after finishing the regular season at 51-31, Chicago lost the seventh game of the division semifinals to Los Angeles by only three points. It was, however, a sign of good things to come.

Norm Van Lier brought the Bulls blazing speed, ferocious defense and the keen ability to spot the open man.

Chet Walker

By 1973-74, Bob Love and Chet Walker had become the top 1-2 scoring punch in the entire NBA. Together, the Bulls stormed to a 54-28 regular season record that year and then powered past the Detroit Pistons in the semifinals. It was Chicago's seventh playoff appearance in eight years, and the team's first playoff series victory. Their next opponent was Chicago's archrival, the Milwaukee Bucks, led by their superstar center Lew Alcindor.

Throughout their history, the Bulls had played second-fiddle to the Bucks in the Midwest Division. The Chicago fans thought it would be different this time, but Alcindor and his skyhook were simply too much. The Bulls were humbled in the Western Conference finals, losing four games to none.

Throughout their history the Bulls had played second-fiddle to the Bucks . . .

"We were extremely demoralized by the sweep," Jerry Sloan would later admit, "but we knew we could bounce back. We had a tough-guy image of ourselves. All we could think about was coming back the next year and getting our revenge."

Actually, the Bulls came limping back the following season. Walker was a step slower, and Boerwinkle was increasingly troubled by chronic knee injuries. To make matters worse, Van Lier and Love both threatened to leave Chicago over salary disputes. In the midst of the chaos, however, Motta helped engineer a trade that brought big Nate Thurmond of Golden State to Chicago. In the opening game of the season, Thurmond blocked an all-time team record 12 shots in leading the Bulls to a 120-115 victory over Atlanta.

Thurmond's incredible debut helped reunite the Bulls. By season's end, they had captured their first division title with a 47-35 record.

After defeating Kansas City in the first round of the 1975 playoffs, the Bulls faced off with Golden State in the conference finals. Chet Walker was hobbled by a bad thigh, but Love and Van Lier took up the scoring

Bob Love

slack. The Warriors began with the homecourt advantage, but the Bulls stole it away and came home with a chance to win the series in six games.

In that sixth game, the Golden State defense all but smothered Chicago's offense, limiting the Bulls to 31 second-half points. Rick Barry reeled off a game-high 36 points, silencing the crowd and sending Chicago down to an 86-72 defeat.

Basically, that loss marked the end of an era in Bulls basketball. Over the next few months, numerous roster changes were made. Chet Walker and Jerry Sloan retired. Nate Thurmond was traded away. The Bulls sank to 24-58 in 1975-76 and failed to make the playoffs for only the second time in their nine-year history. To top it all off, coach Motta was fired, leaving everyone on the shores of Lake Michigan wondering what would happen next.

On June 17, 1976, the American Basketball Association officially closed its doors. For nine years the ABA had tried to coexist with the NBA. Now, having finally admitted defeat, the ABA merged four of its teams with the NBA and released the remaining ABA players to a special dispersal draft.

The Warriors began with the homecourt advantage, but the Bulls stole it away and came home with a chance to win the series. . .

By the 1973-74 season, Chet Walker (25) and Bob Love had become the top 1-2 scoring punch in the entire NBA.

The Bulls claimed one of the biggest prizes in this draft, 7-foot-2 center Artis Gilmore. Chicago paid $1 million for Gilmore, and it was money well-spent. While he didn't appear to be particularly fast or agile, he was a complete player.

In college, Artis averaged 20 points and 20 rebounds per game, leading the Jacksonville Dolphins to a 27-2 record his senior year. Gilmore was a dominant player in the ABA. He was the leading rebounder in four out of the five years he spent in the league. Gilmore was also the ABA's Rookie of the Year and a perennial All-Star.

Artis was a welcome addition to the Bulls, a team that was still in a state of confusion over the discouraging events of the previous two seasons. Ed Badger, Motta's assistant, had moved up to head coach for the 1976-77 season, but the team started slowly under his leadership. At one point, the Bulls suffered through a 13-game losing streak, their longest ever in franchise history, but

While he didn't appear to be particularly fast or agile, he was a complete player.

then Gilmore caught fire.

Teamed up with Mickey Johnson and rookie Scott May on the frontline, and supported by Van Lier and Wilbur Holland in the backcourt, Gilmore was outstanding on both ends of the court. He averaged over 18 points per game and blocked over 200 shots, leading the Bulls back to the playoffs.

Artis Gilmore, a superb defensive player, set single-game records of 25 defensive rebounds and 11 blocked shots for Chicago in 1977-78.

The team's success continued through the first round of the 1977 playoffs. The Bulls, however, fell in three games to Bill Walton and the eventual NBA champion Portland Trail Blazers.

Despite this encouraging performance, the Bulls, hampered by injuries, suffered through two mediocre seasons before appointing Jerry Sloan as coach at the end of the 1979 season.

As a player, Sloan had given the Bulls all-out intensity and he expected the same from the team as their coach. "If there's a loose ball and nobody goes for it, I don't care if the score is 100-50, I'm going to come down on somebody hard," Sloan promised fans.

Over the next two seasons, coach Sloan assembled the most intimidating lineup in the NBA. In the backcourt stood 6-foot-7 Bobby Wilkerson and 6-foot-8 Reggie Theus. Reggie had made the All-Rookie team in 1978-79 and was about to wrest the Bulls' high-scoring honors from Artis Gilmore. At forward stood 6-foot-9 Larry Kenon and 6-foot-9 David Greenwood, with 7-foot-2 Gilmore in the middle.

Give the big guys credit. After moving to the Eastern Conference in 1980-81, Jerry Sloan's Bulls took second place in the division with a 45-37 regular season record. This was the club's most wins in six years and their first playoff berth since 1977. They defeated the New York Knicks 2-0 in the first round. And even though the Bulls were swept 4-0 in the second round by Larry Bird and the eventual world champion Boston Celtics, Chicago was voted the NBA's Best Turnaround Club.

■

Reggie Theus came out of nowhere to make the NBA All-Rookie team in the 1978-79 season.

The following season, the Bulls had a chance to prove they were something other than a one man team when Jordan was sidelined with a broken foot for 64 games. Though rookie forward Charles Oakley set several rebounding records during Jordan's absence, the Bulls generally appeared lost until Jordan returned in time to lead them back into the NBA playoffs.

Jordan scored an NBA playoff record 63 points in a single game against the Boston Celtics, but the Bulls were still eliminated in three games. It was then that the Chicago front office fired Stan Albeck, who had coached the Bulls for just one season, and hired former Philadelphia 76ers guard Doug Collins to take over as head coach.

It appeared that Collins' leadership was just what the Bulls needed. He knew how to get every bit of talent out of his team. The Bulls finished that season at 40-42, their best record in six years, thanks once again to Michael Jordan. He averaged 37.1 points, recorded 236 steals and blocked 125 shots. To put those statistics in perspective,

He became the first player in NBA history to lead the league in both scoring . . . and steals.

consider that Jordan scored more points than his next three teammates combined.

Jordan continued his phenomenal play the following year, 1987-88. He became the first player in NBA history to lead the league in both scoring, 35 points per game, and steals, 3.16 per game. Jordan also blocked over 130 shots. To cap off his incredible season, Michael was named the NBA's Defensive Player of the Year, as well as the league's Most Valuable Player. Among other honors, Jordan was also the Slam Dunk Champion, the leading vote-getter for the All-Star game and the game's MVP.

■

On September 12, 1984 Chicago announced the signing of No. 1 draft pick Michael "Air" Jordan, heralded in the press as "a stick of dynamite in Nikes."

His extraordinary talents were marvelled at outside the NBA as well. Baseball's Roger Craig, manager of the San Francisco Giants, said Jordan would be a welcome addition to his ballclub. "I'd put him in centerfield," Craig said. "He could jump into the second deck to catch home runs. He could hit for power. He'd be like Willie Mays, a guy who can do everything. He's the best athlete I've ever seen."

With his amazing play, Jordan sparked the Bulls to a 50-32 record and the team advanced to the second round of the playoffs for the first time in seven years.

During the first round of the playoffs, Jordan scored 50 and 55 points versus the Cleveland Cavaliers, thus becoming the first player in league history to score 50 or more points in consecutive playoff games.

Although Jordan was without question the key to Chicago's success, there were signs that the Bulls were becoming more than just a one man team.

Third year forward Charles Oakley had a stellar collegiate career at Virginia Union, averaging 24 points and over 17 rebounds per game. At 6-foot-9 and 245 pounds, he is widely considered one of the top defensive players in the NBA. He averaged 13 rebounds per game during the 1987-88 season, ranking second in the league. Rookies Horace Grant, from Clemson University, and Scottie Pippen, out of the University of Central Arkansas, also show promise. Both demonstrated improved play during the stretch drive to the playoffs, where the Bulls were eliminated by the Detroit Pistons. During the off-season, Chicago moved to bolster their roster by trading Oakely to the New York Knicks in exchange for 7-foot-1 center Bill Cartwright.

The Chicago Bulls are without a doubt one of the league's most electrifying teams. With the sensational Michael Jordan and his teammates plugged into the city's energy, the Bulls are sure to be playoff contenders in the years to come.